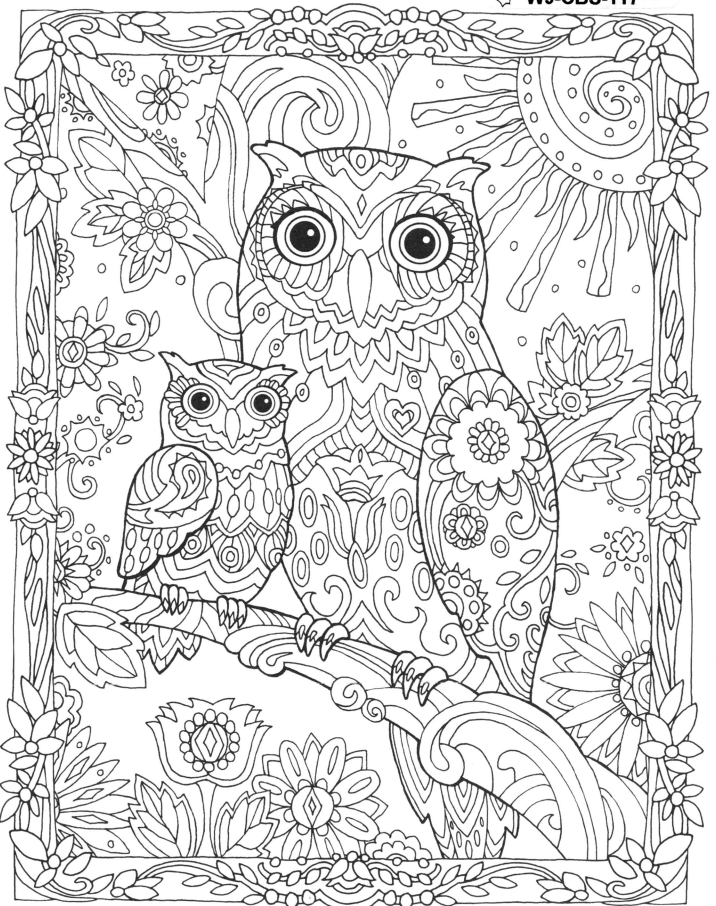

OWLS

COLORING BOOK

MARJORIE SARNAT

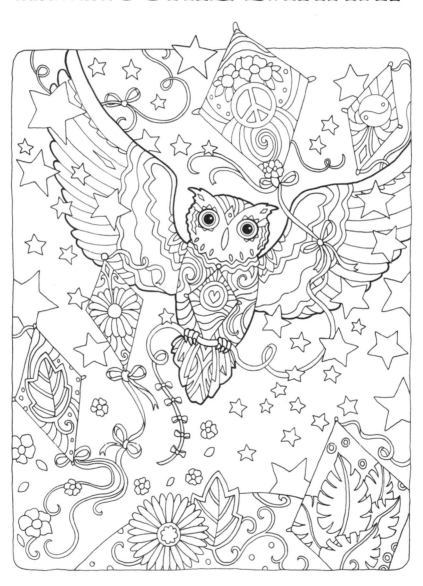

DOVER PUBLICATIONS, INC.
MINEOLA, NEW YORK

Featuring more than thirty ornate owls adorned with everything from tribal patterns and flowers, to peace signs and pirate accessories, this collection will satisfy the colorist and owl enthusiast alike. The latest addition to Dover's *Creative Haven* series for the experienced colorist, the detailed designs provide endless opportunity for experimentation with color and technique. Plus, the imaginative background patterns, scenery, and borders give each plate a polished appearance. Once you are satisfied with your work, the perforated, unbacked pages allow for easy display.

Copyright
Copyright © 2015 by Marjorie Sarnat
All rights reserved.

Bibliographical Note
Owls Coloring Book is a new work,
first published by Dover Publications, Inc., in 2015.

International Standard Book Number
ISBN-13: 978-0-486-79664-2
ISBN-10: 0-486-79664-7

Manufactured in the United States by RR Donnelley
79664709   2015
www.doverpublications.com

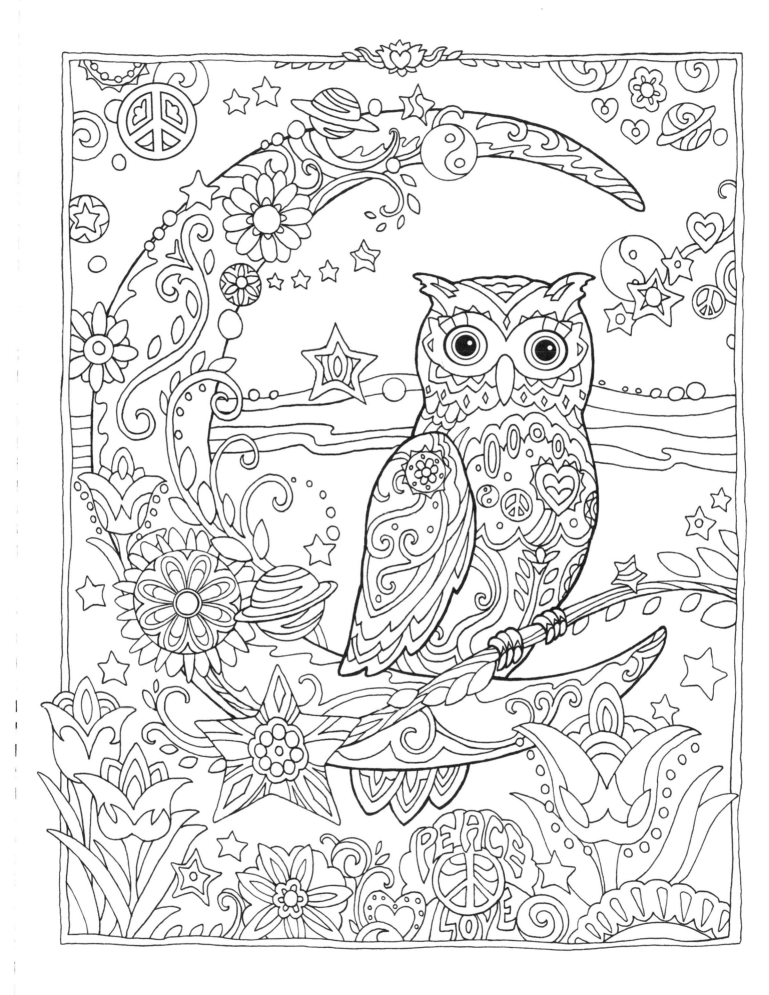

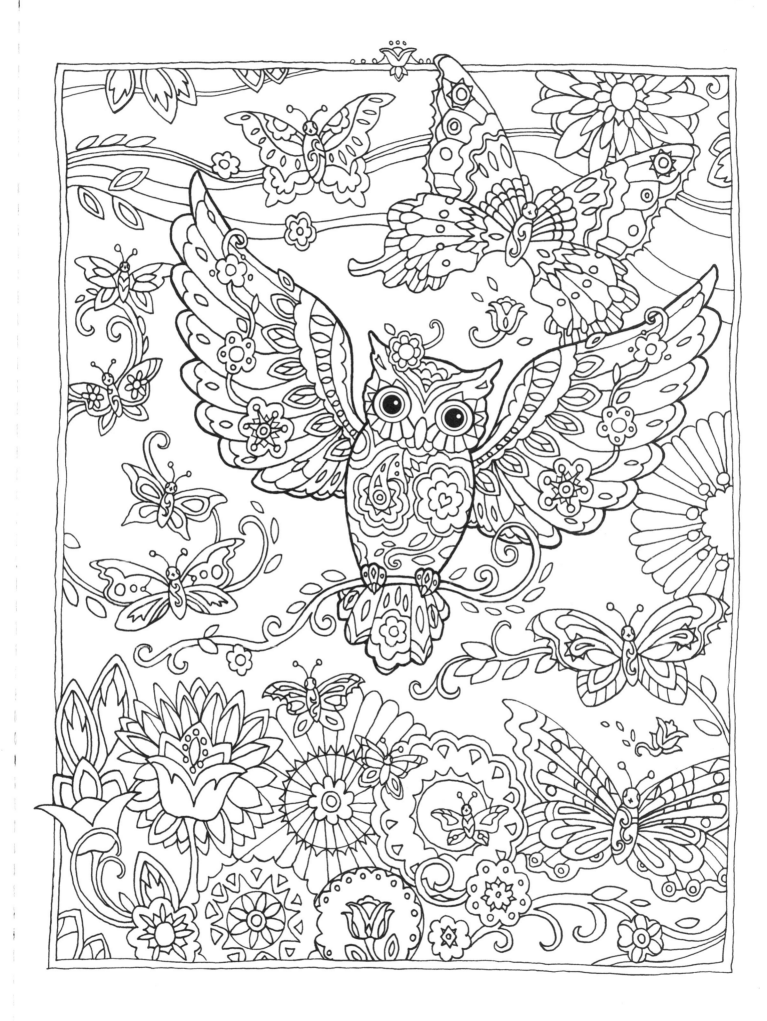

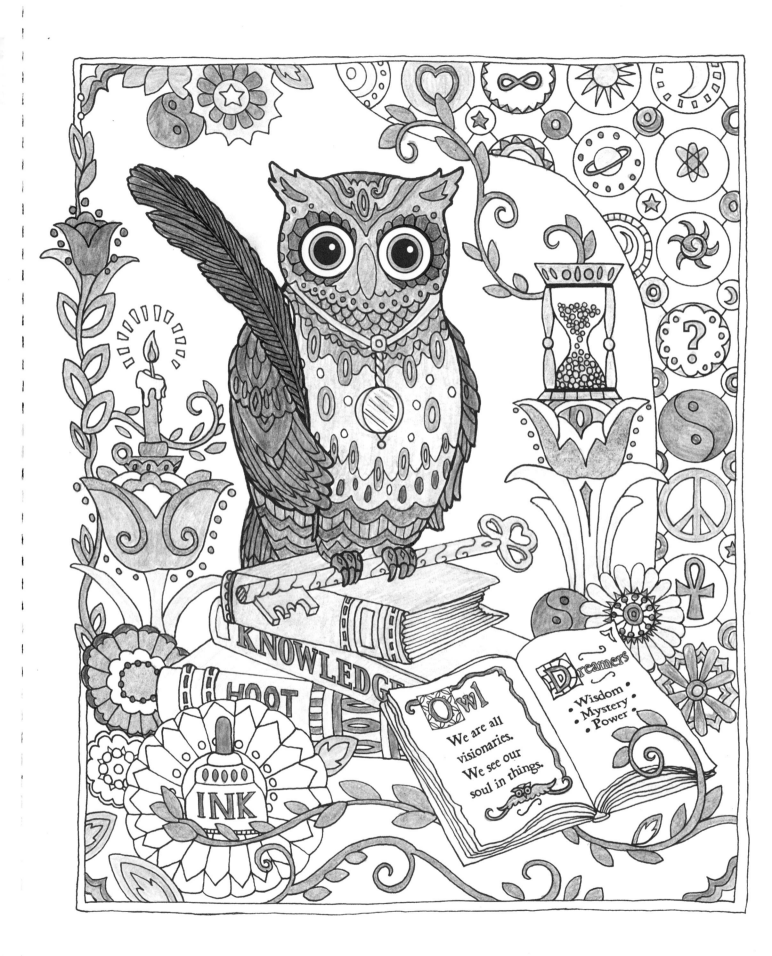

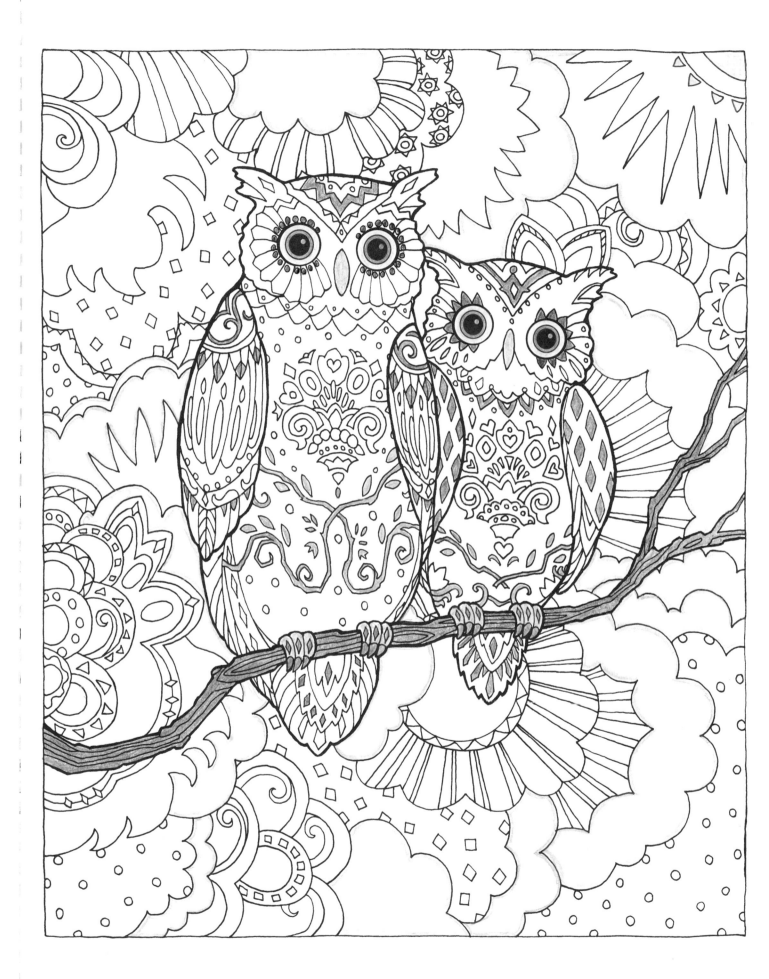

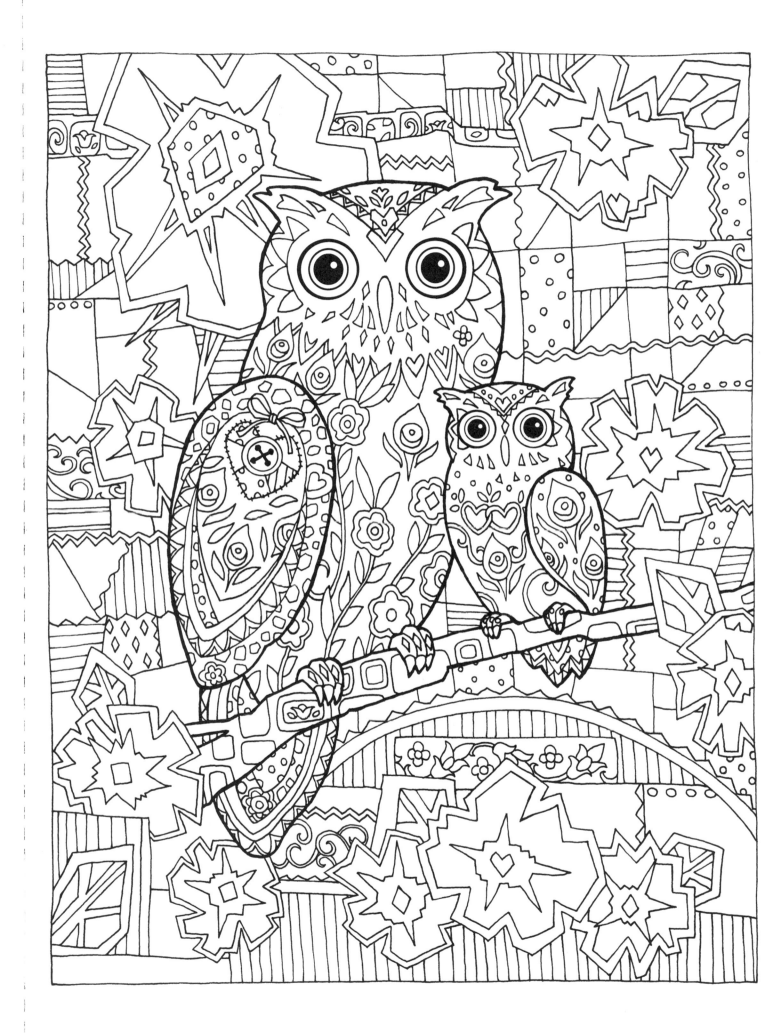

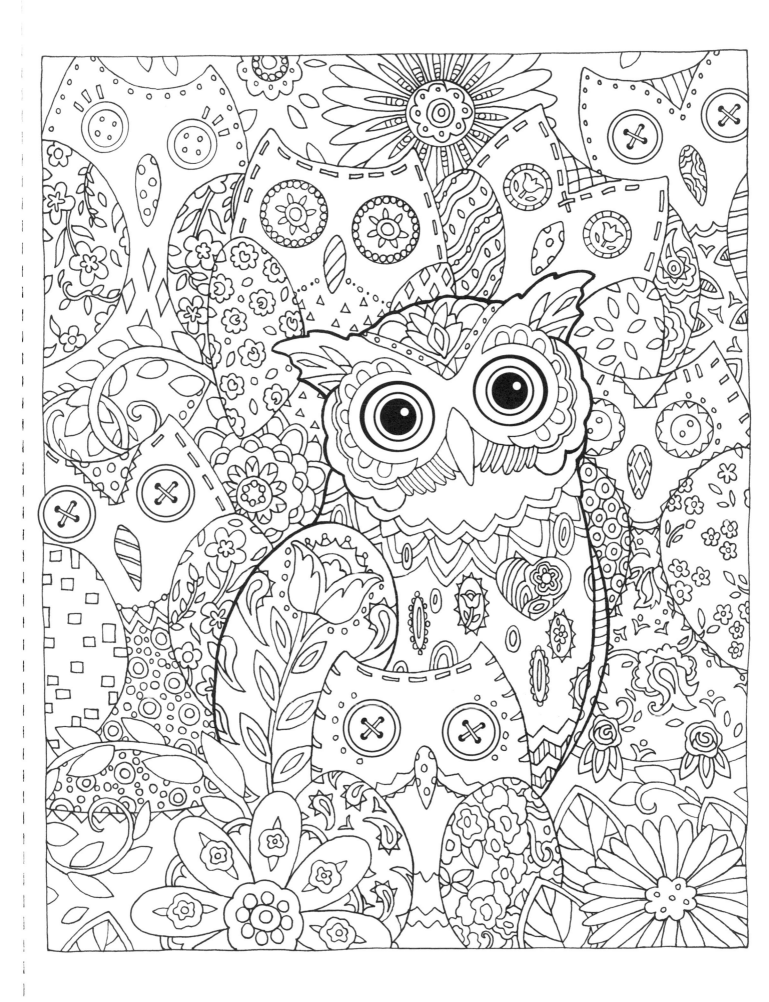

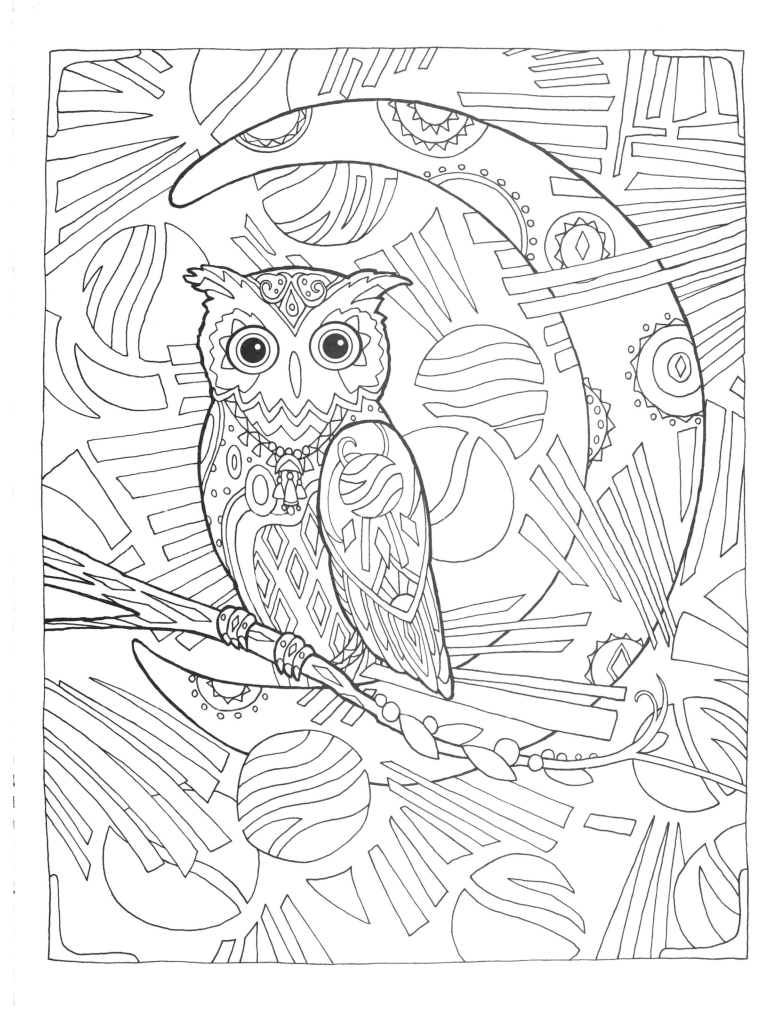

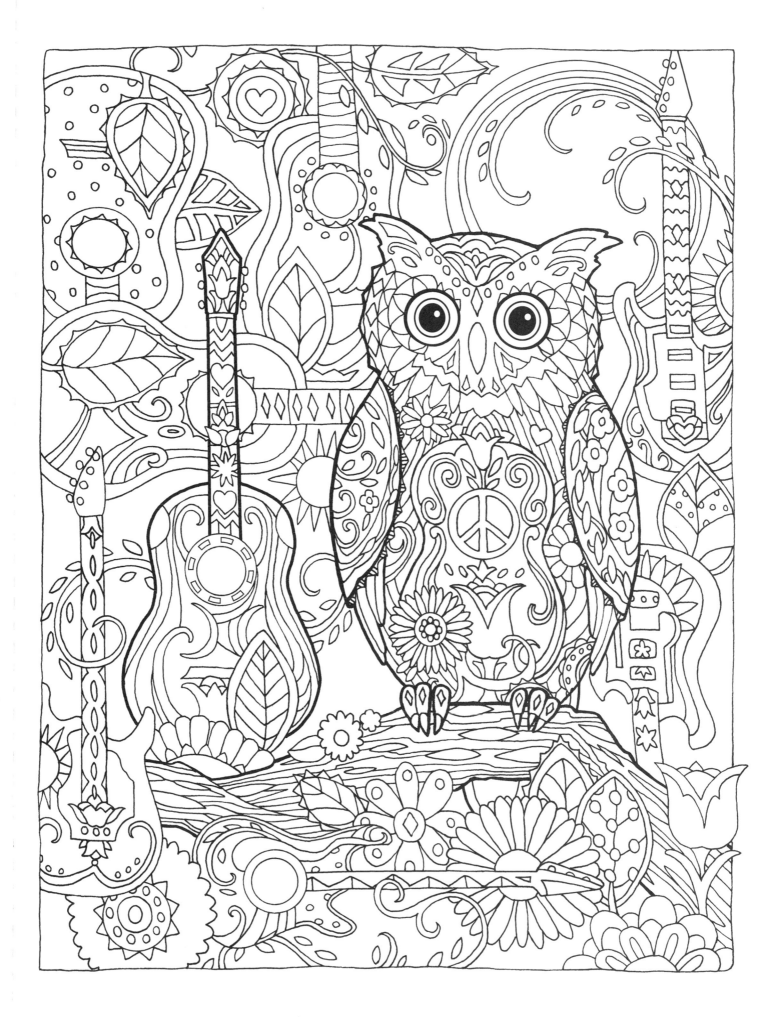

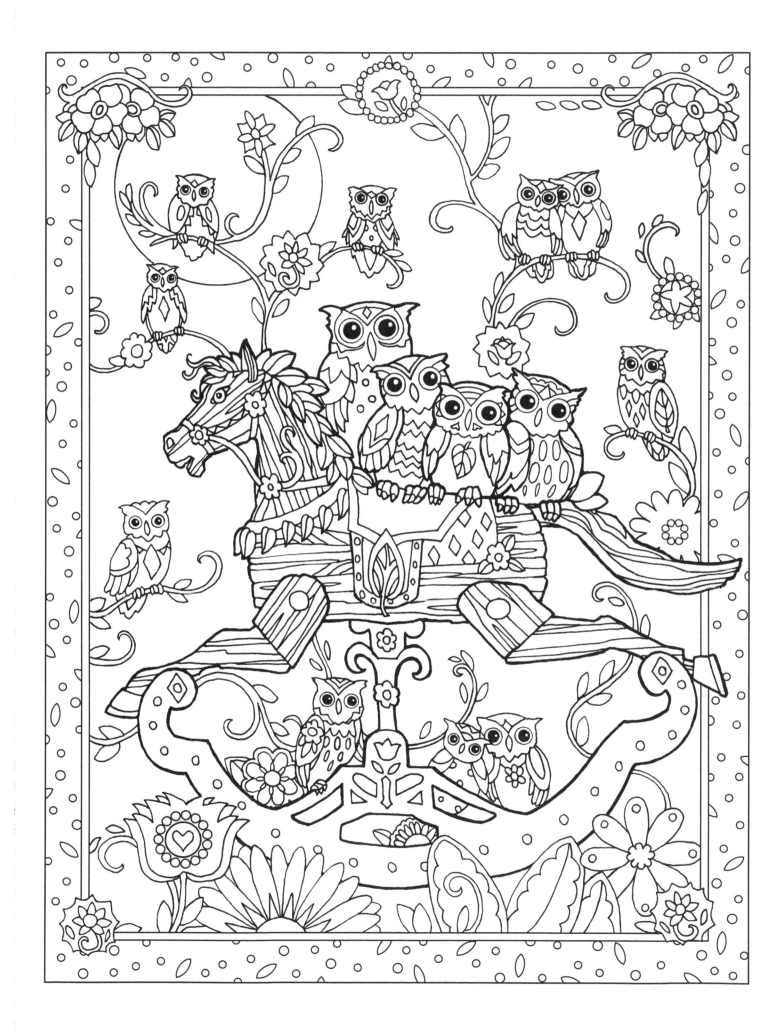

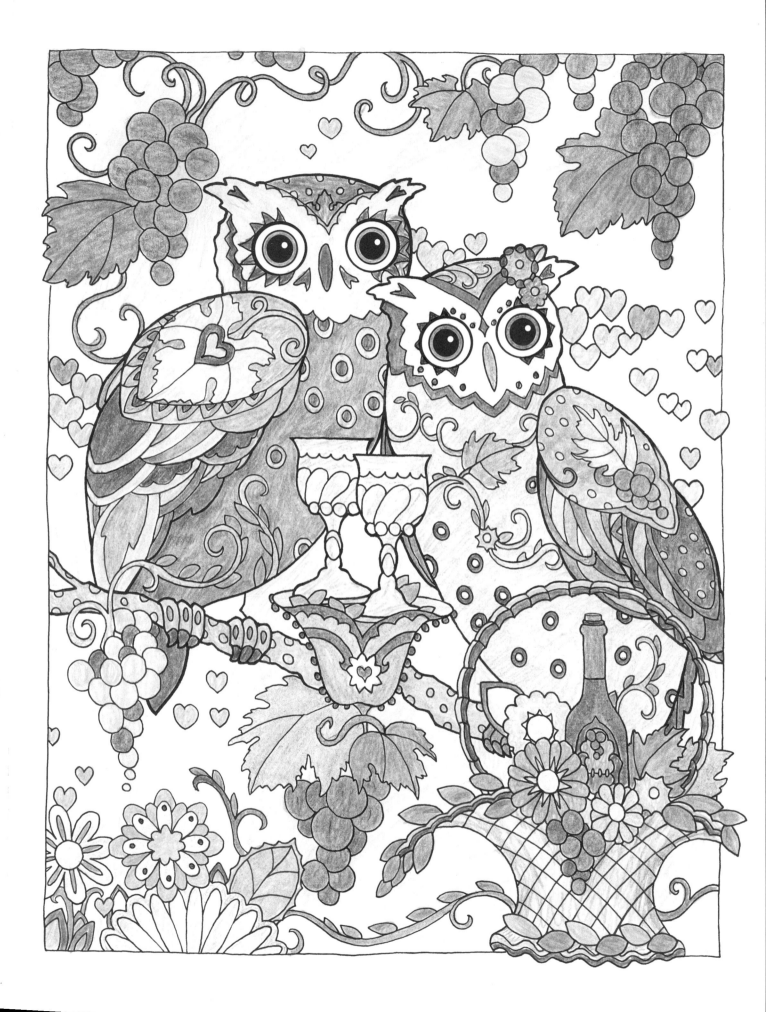

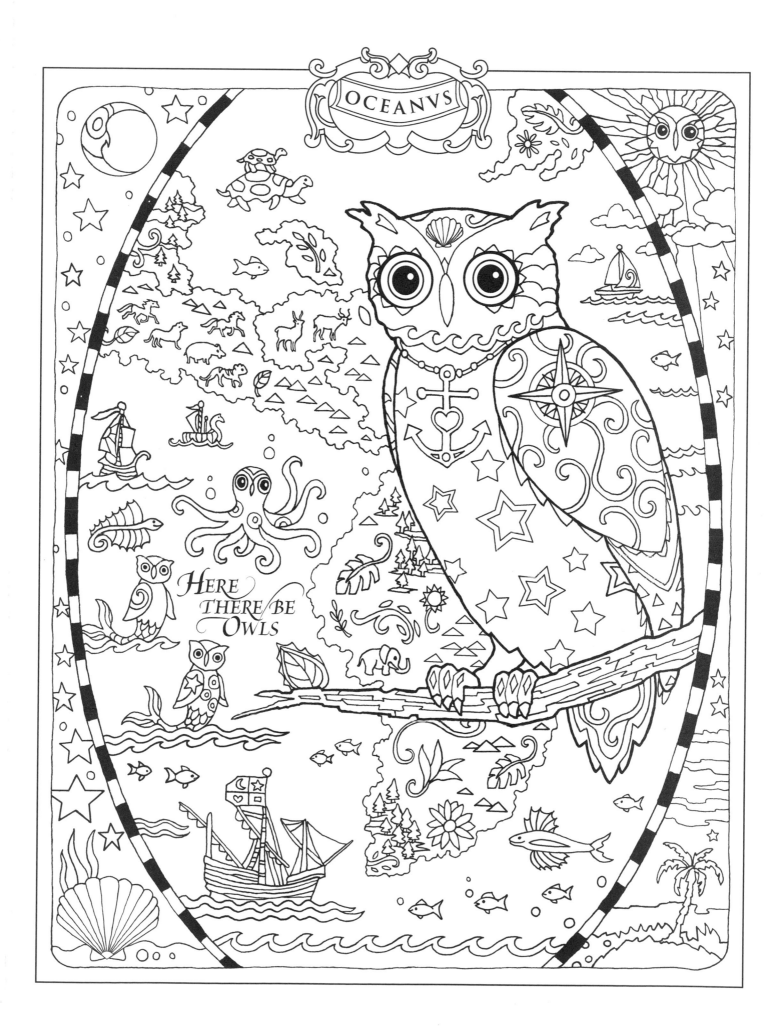

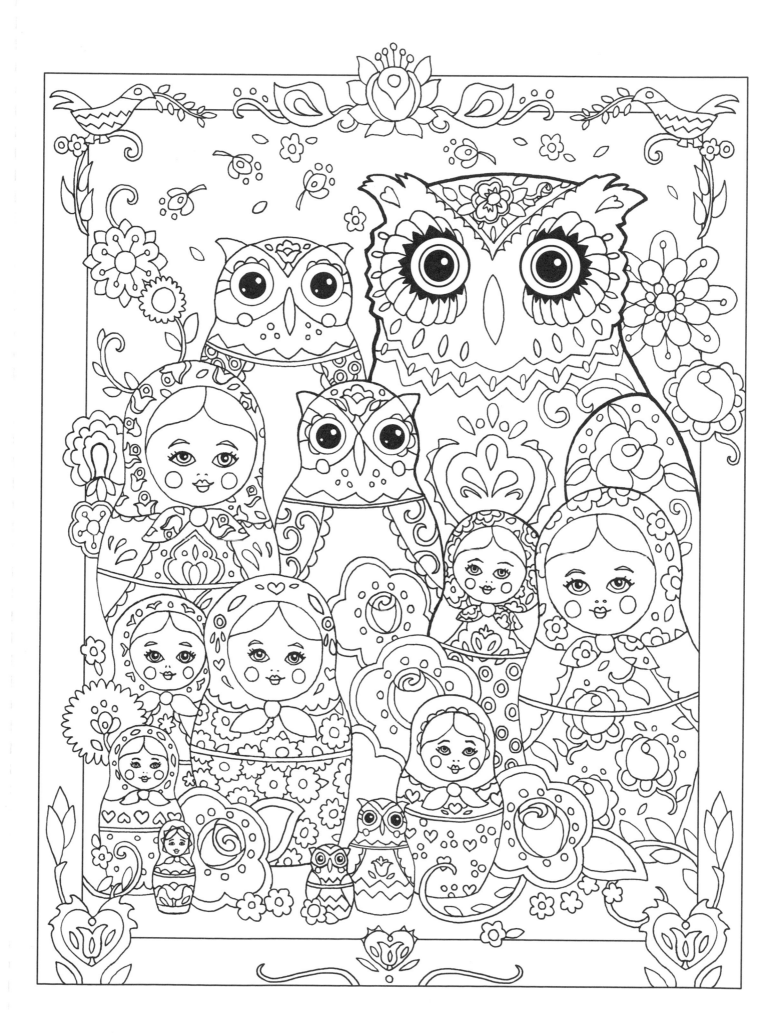

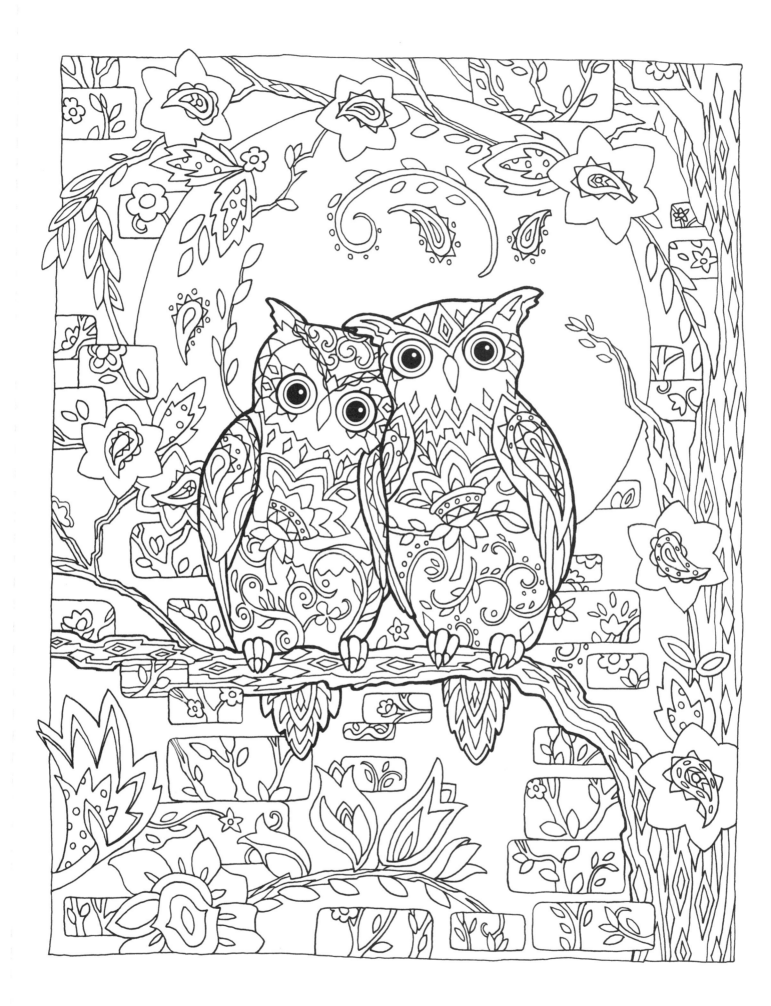

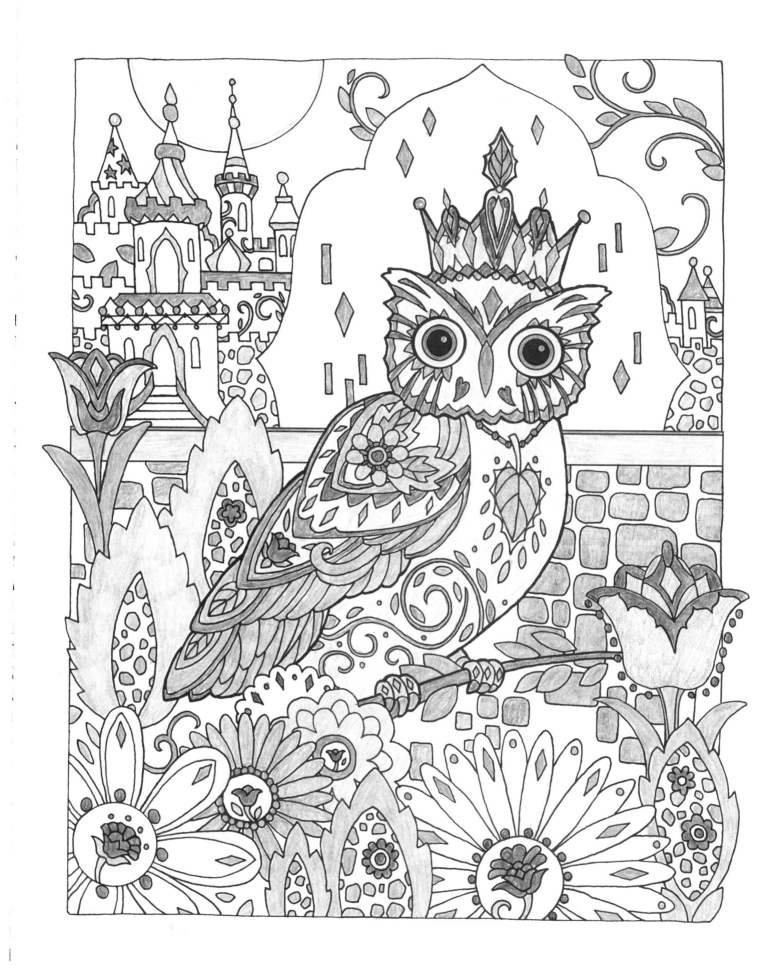

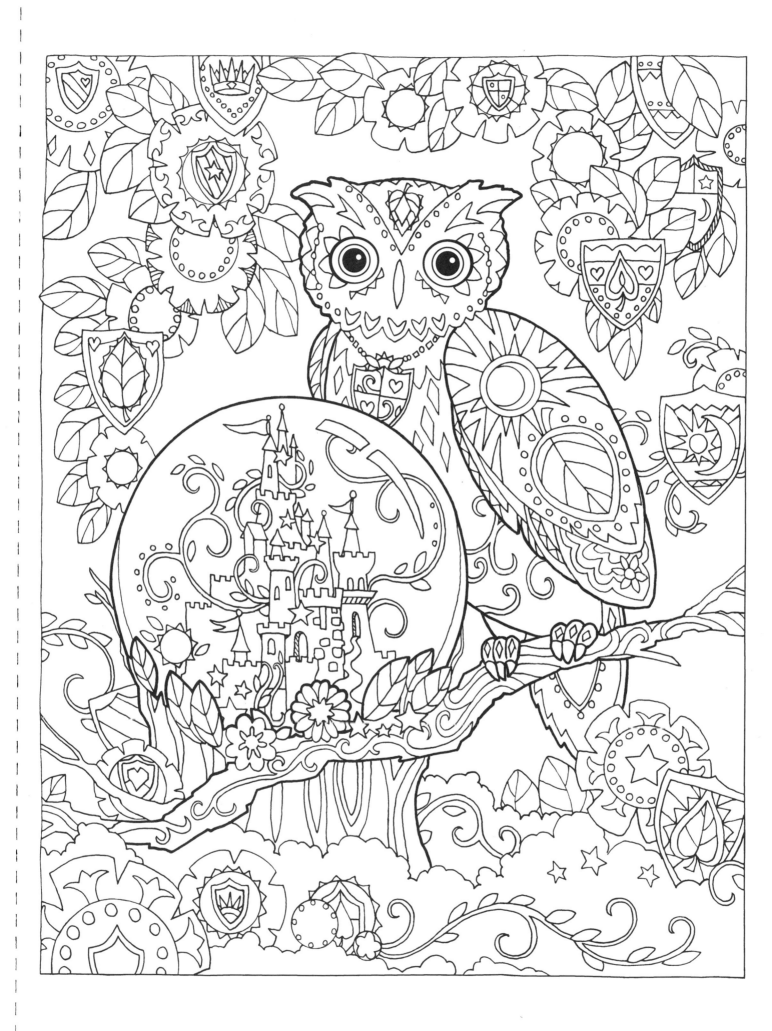

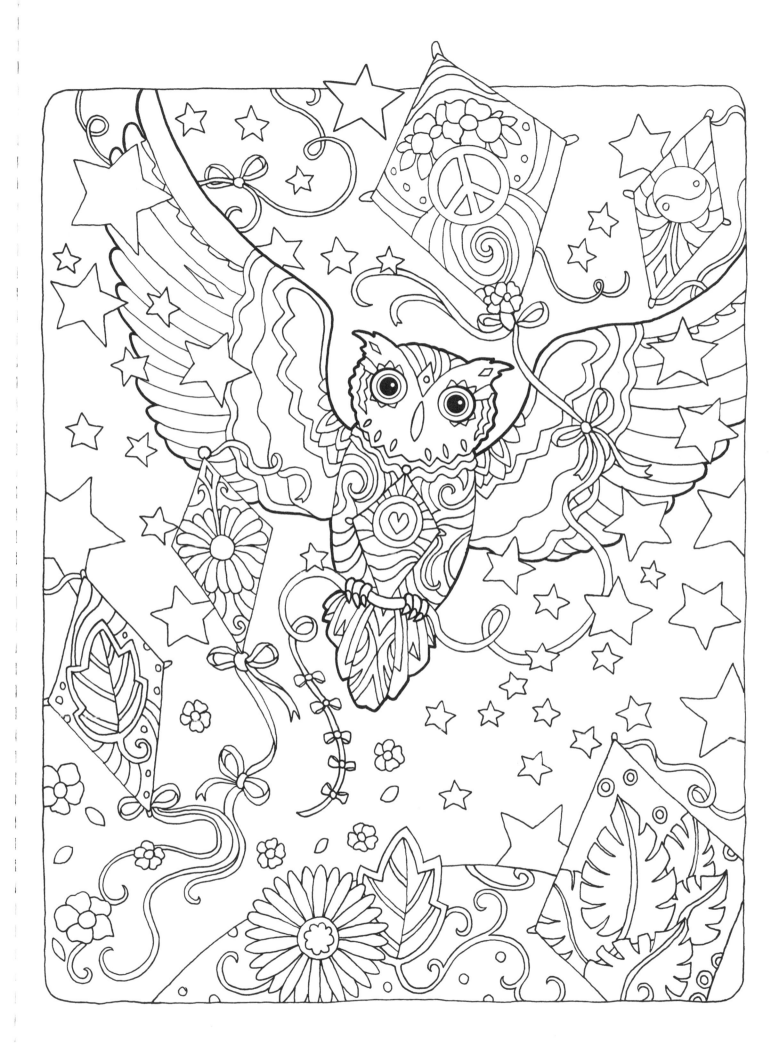

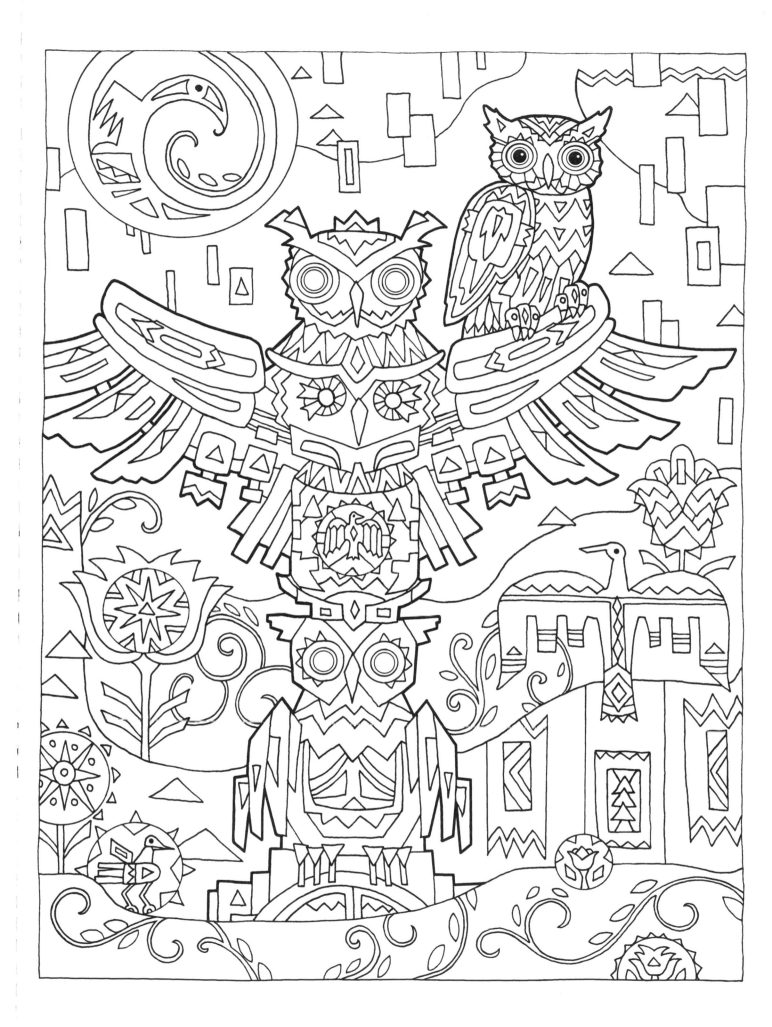

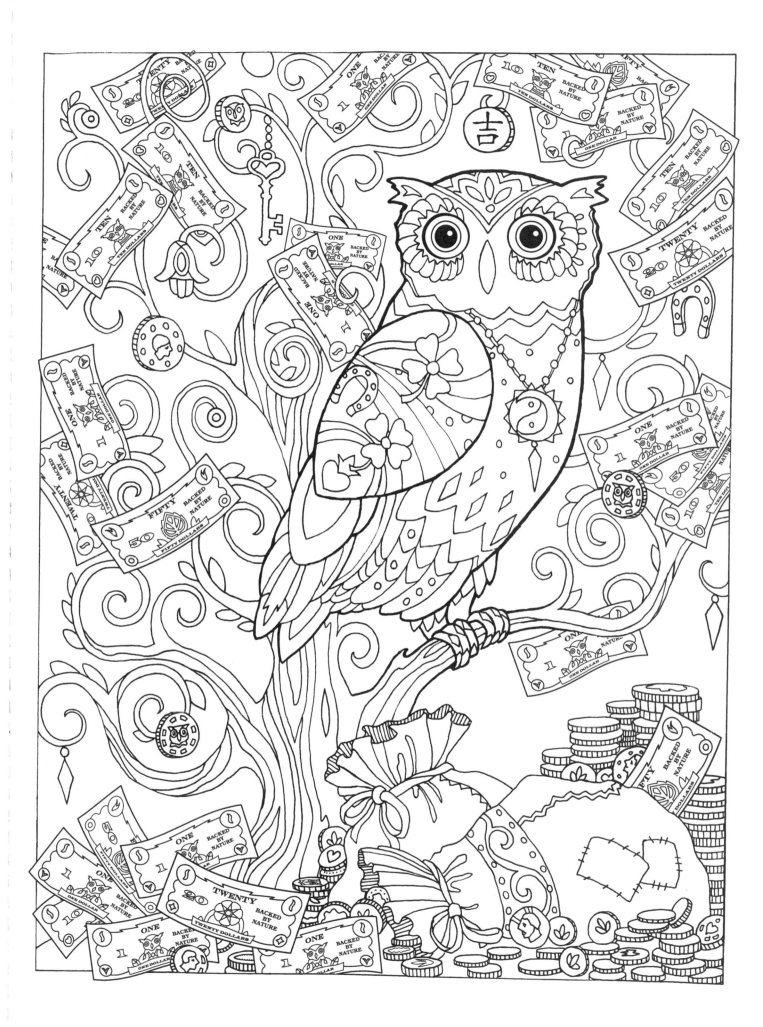

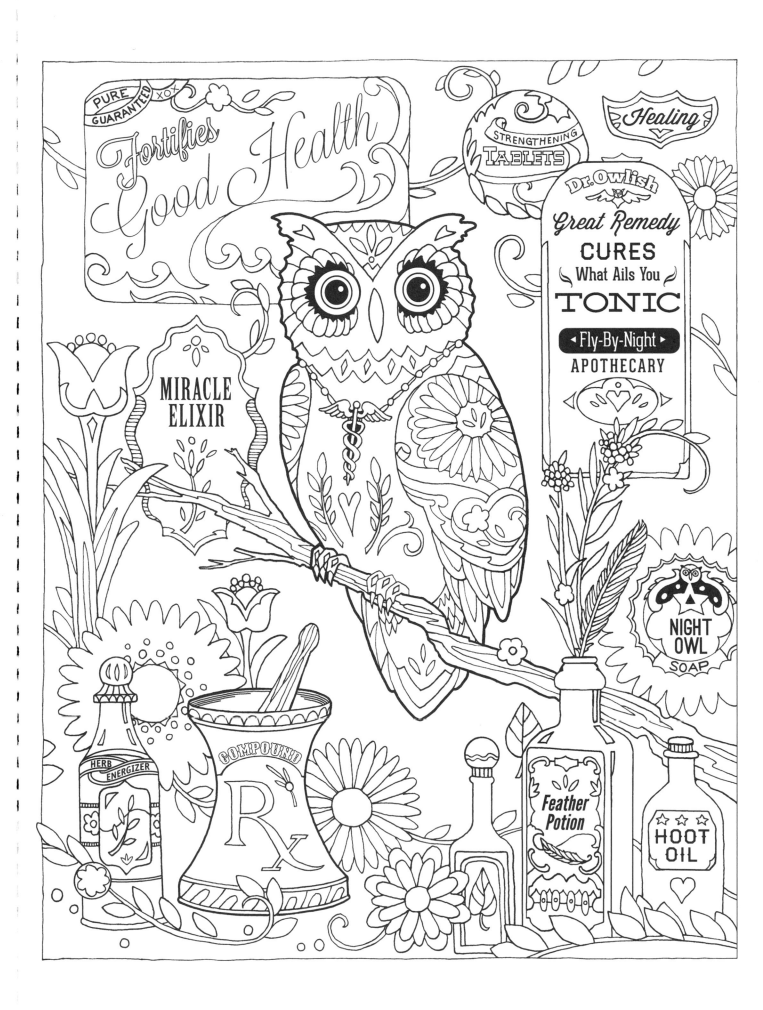

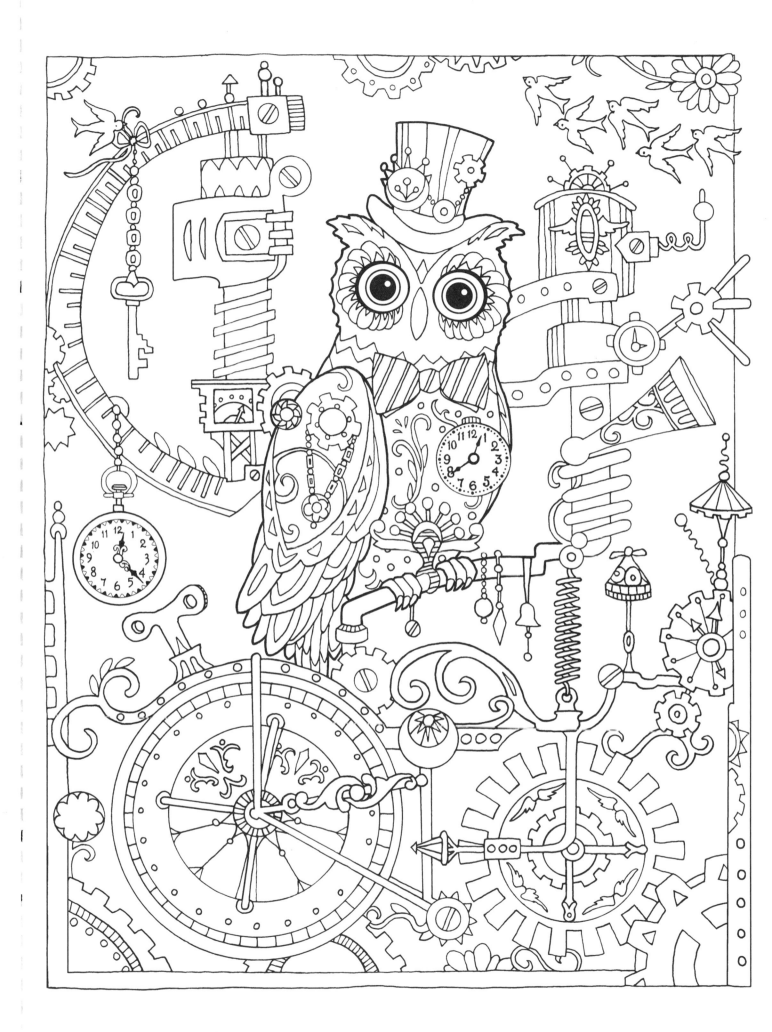

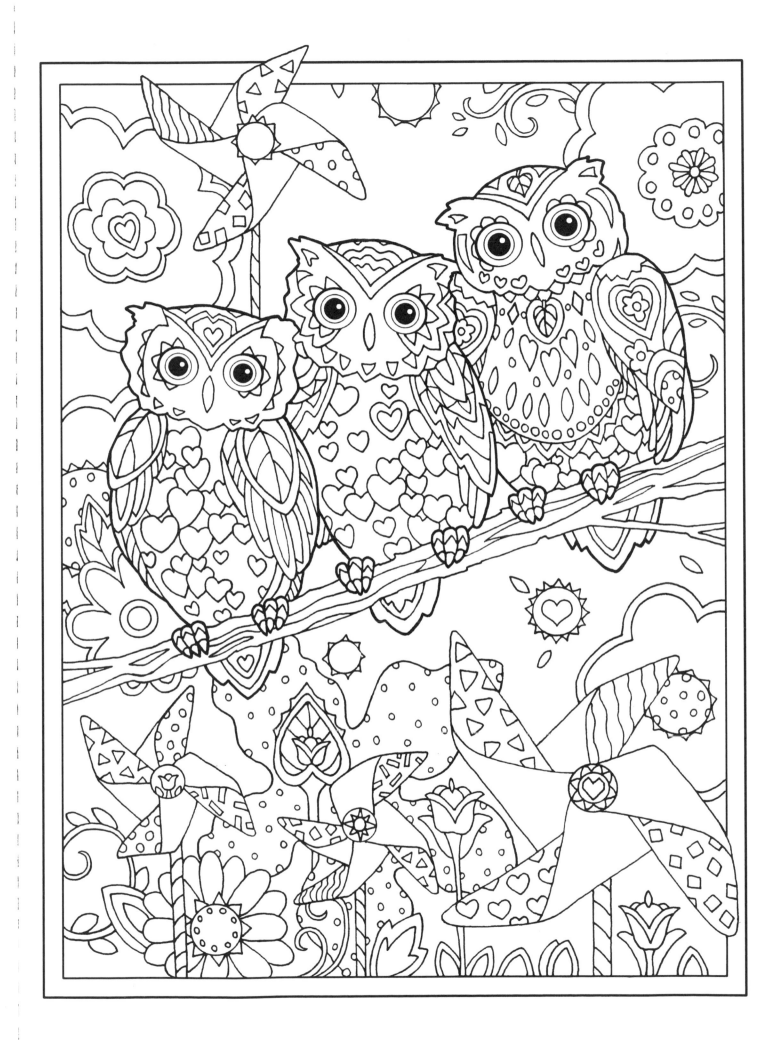

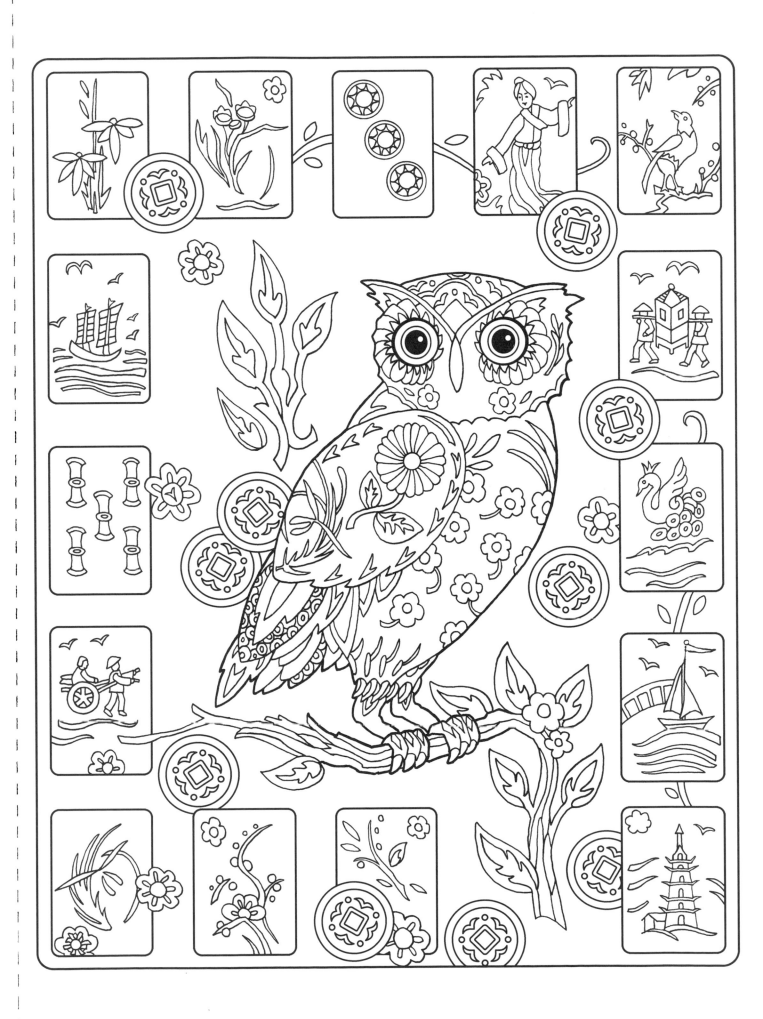

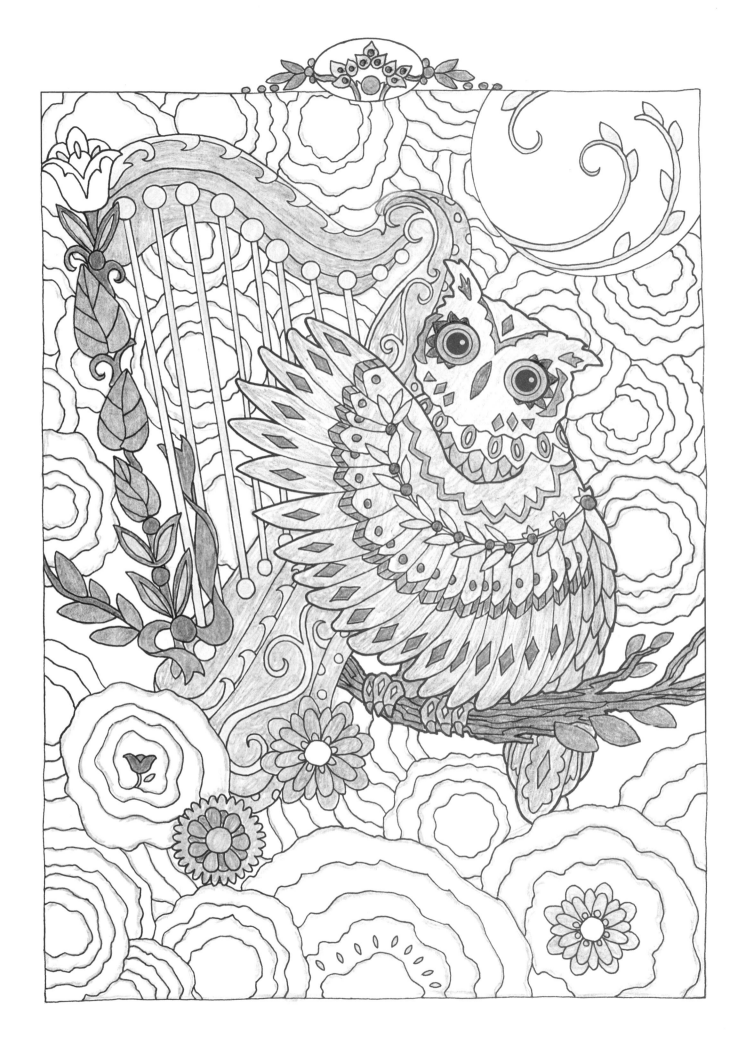

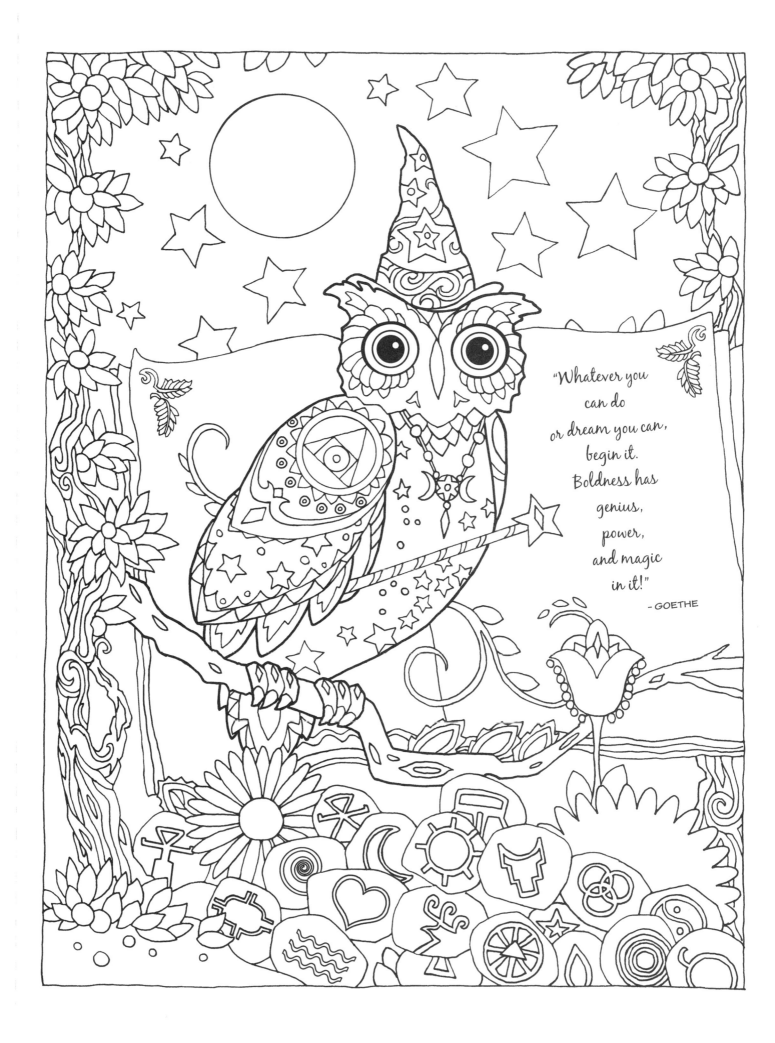

"Whatever you can do or dream you can, begin it. Boldness has genius, power, and magic in it!"

— GOETHE

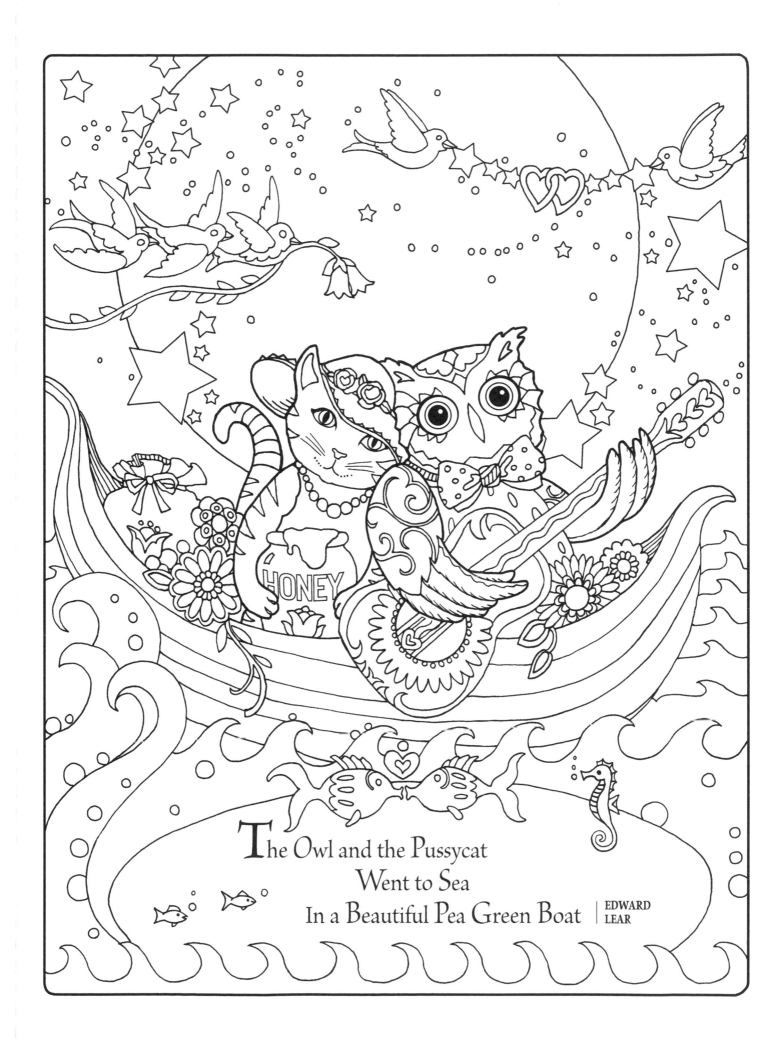

The Owl and the Pussycat
Went to Sea
In a Beautiful Pea Green Boat | EDWARD LEAR

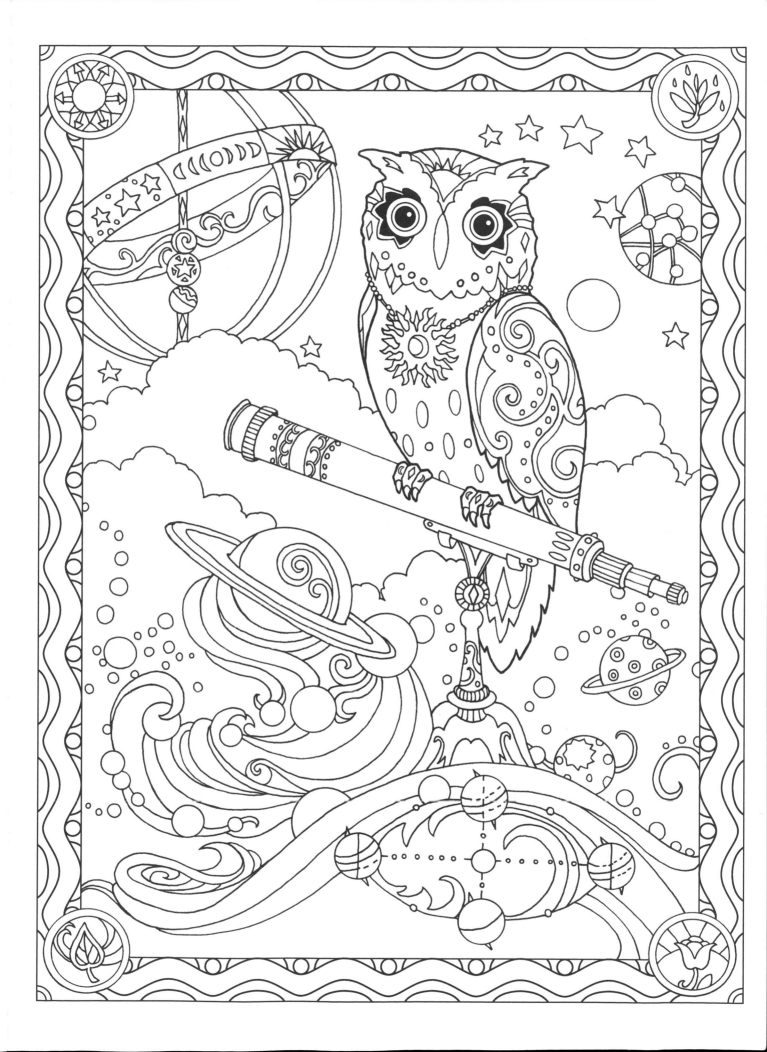

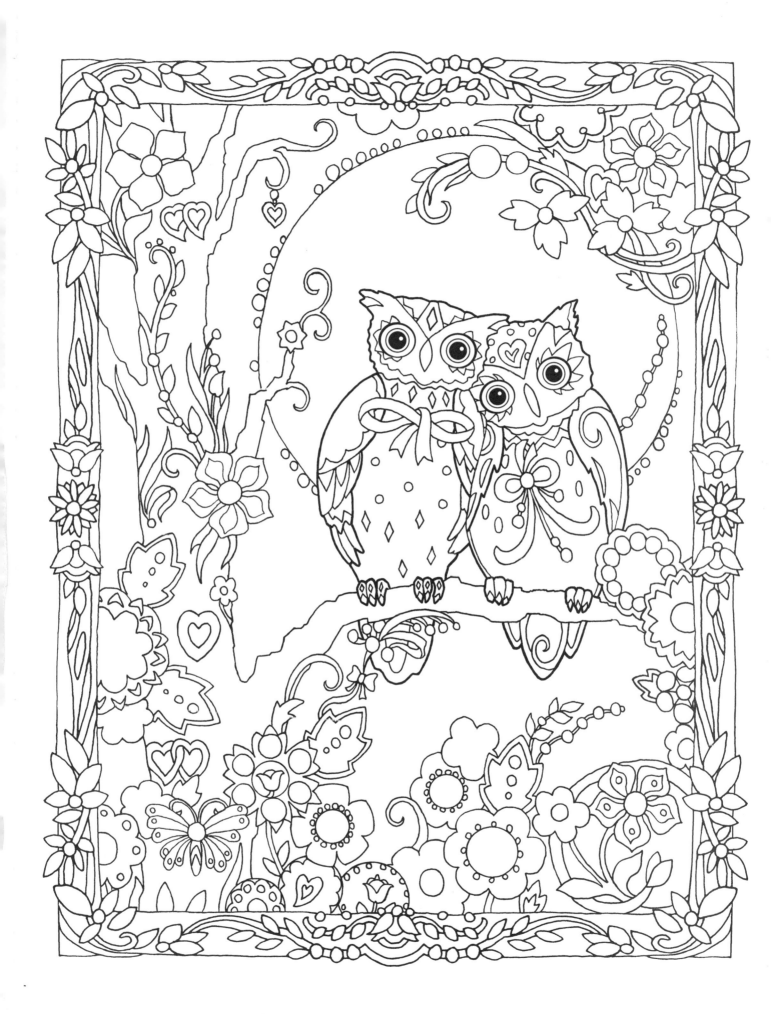

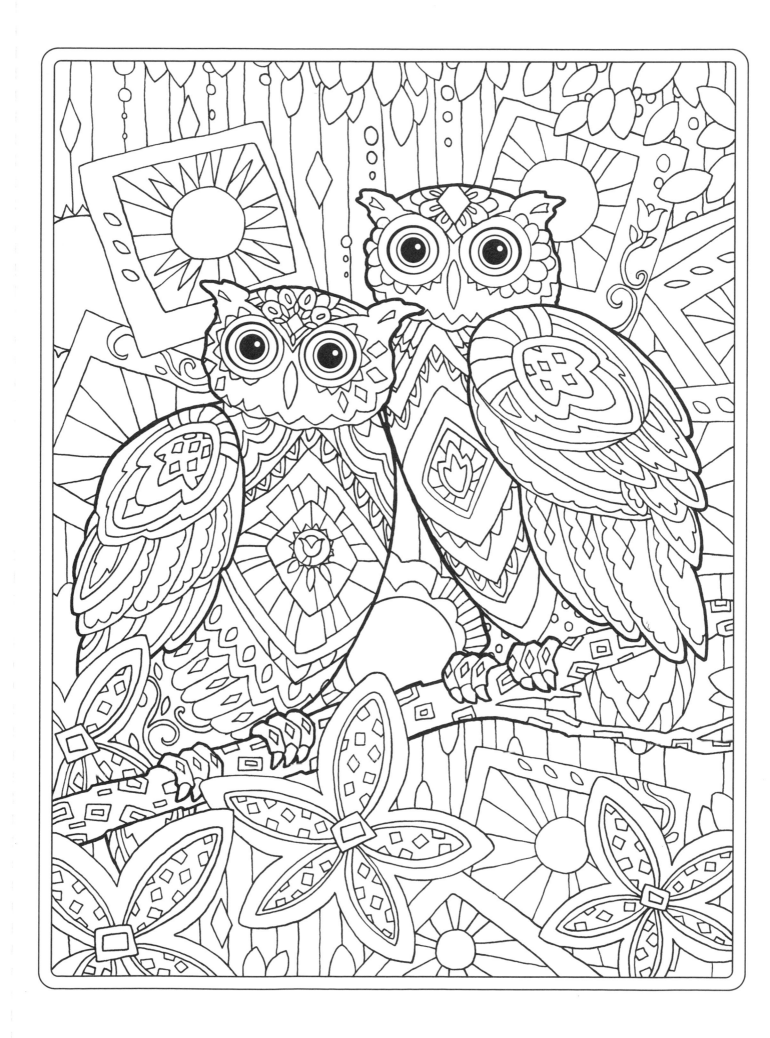

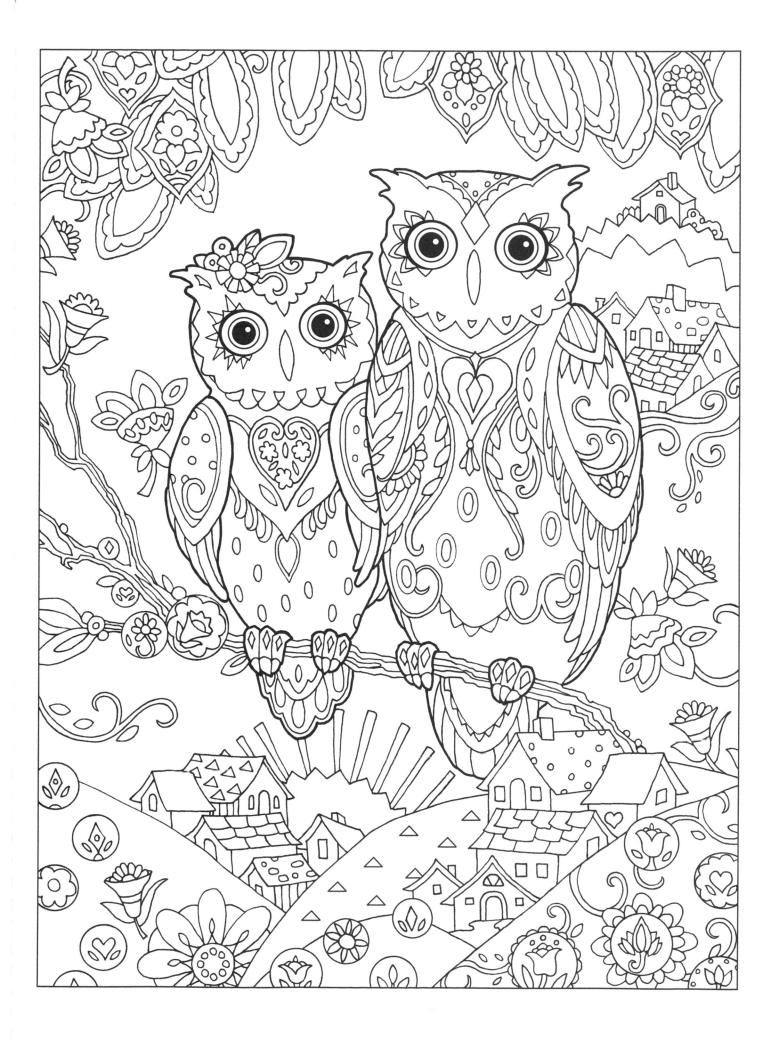

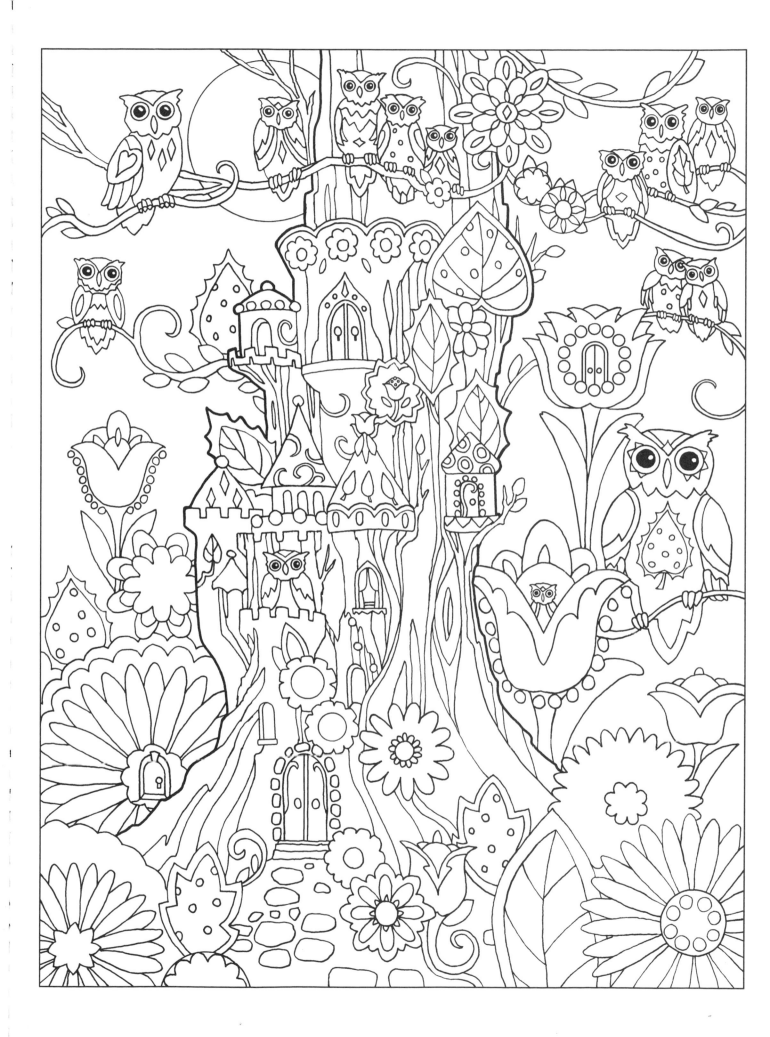